PLEASE, Mind the Bear

MNS PRESS

PLEASE, Mind the Bear

Michelle Nelson-Schmidt

Copyright © 2022 by Michelle Nelson-Schmidt.

All rights reserved. No part of this publication may be reproduced, distributed or transmitted in any form or by any means, including photocopying, recording, or other electronic or mechanical methods, without the prior written permission of the publisher, except in the case of brief quotations embodied in critical reviews and certain other noncommercial uses permitted by copyright law. For permission requests, write to the publisher, addressed "Attention: Permissions Coordinator," at the email below.

Michelle Nelson-Schmidt/MNS PRESS
Perdido Key, Florida 32507
www.MNScreative.com | books@MNScreative.com

Author: Michelle Nelson-Schmidt
Title: Mind the Bear/Michelle Nelson-Schmidt
Description: First edition. | Florida: MNS PRESS, 2022
ISBN Hardback: 978-1-952013-62-1
ISBN Paperback: 978-1-952013-63-8

Text Copyright ©Michelle Nelson-Schmidt, 2022
Illustration Copyright ©Michelle Nelson-Schmidt, 2022

Perdido Key / Michelle Nelson-Schmidt — First Edition
Printed in the United States of America

For all of us. May we see each other's boundaries and respect them.

Deep in the forest, in a house made of stone,
a brown grizzly bear lived all alone.

He'd hike, cook, and read to fill up his days.
He was fine by himself. He preferred it that way.

He didn't ask much of his neighbors out there.
"Just leave me alone. Just please - Mind the Bear."

He thought it was simple, he thought it was fine.
The message was clear, it was all on the sign.

You see, Rabbit did what Rabbit wanted to do,

regardless of what others wanted him to.

"Mind the bear, mind the bear," he said with a scowl.

But Rabbit kept pushing, ignoring Bear's words, acting as if Bear's words were not heard.

Finally Bear stopped and glared Rabbit's way.
"This is the last time I'll ask you, please do as I say."

Maybe Rabbit didn't care, or thought it a joke,
because he picked up the stick and gave Bear a POKE.

That was the moment Rabbit found out one should care,
if you ignore all requests and don't mind a bear.

Bear stood on two legs, he got giant and tall.
His mouth got real big and his eyes got real small.

The sky seemed to darken, Rabbit's eyes opened wide.
The birds and the bees looked for places to hide.

Bear's words exploded like lightning and fire. They shot out at Rabbit who caused all this ire.

No one's sure what happened to Rabbit that day.
Perhaps he said sorry and just hopped away.

I don't know about you, but I know that I'll care,
the next time I'm told to please mind a bear.

(No rabbits were harmed in the making of this book. -MNS)

A few questions for you from the author

Did you know what 'Mind the Bear' meant before you read the book? If not, what do you think it means now?

When do you think Rabbit should have minded Bear's rules?

Why do you think Bear got so angry?

Consequences are what happen as a result of your actions. What do you think Rabbit's consequences were for not minding Bear's rules? What do you think happened to Rabbit at the end?

What could Rabbit have done differently?

What could Bear have done differently?

Do you have rules for yourself that you would like people to mind? What are your rules?

Thank you for reading my book! I hope you loved it as much as I loved creating it for you!

Michelle Nilson-Schmidt

CPSIA information can be obtained
at www.ICGtesting.com
Printed in the USA
JSHW040321270222
R11466000004B/R114660PG23327JSX00010B/3